Pin It!

Pinterest Projects for the Real World

Carolyn Bernhardt

**Checkerboard
Library**

An Imprint of Abdo Publishing
abdopublishing.com

abdopublishing.com

Published by Abdo Publishing, a division of ABDO, PO Box 398166, Minneapolis, Minnesota 55439. Copyright © 2017 by Abdo Consulting Group, Inc. International copyrights reserved in all countries. No part of this book may be reproduced in any form without written permission from the publisher. Checkerboard Library™ is a trademark and logo of Abdo Publishing.

Printed in the United States of America, North Mankato, Minnesota

062016
092016

Content Developer: Nancy Tuminelly
Design and Production: Mighty Media, Inc.
Series Editor: Liz Salzmann
Photo Credits: AP Images; Conor McCabe Photography; Getty Images; Mighty Media, Inc.; Shutterstock

The following manufacturers/names appearing in this book are trademarks: Crayola®, DecoColor™, Elmer's®, Sharpie®

Publishers Cataloging-in-Publication Data
Names: Bernhardt, Carolyn, author.
Title: Pin it! : Pinterest projects for the real world / by Carolyn Bernhardt.
Description: Minneapolis, MN : Abdo Publishing, [2017] | Series: Cool social
    media | Includes bibliographical references and index.
Identifiers: LCCN 2016936498 | ISBN 9781680783575 (lib. bdg.) |
    ISBN 9781680790252 (ebook)
Subjects: LCSH: Pinterest--Juvenile literature. | Internet marketing--Juvenile
    literature. | Photography--Digital techniques--Juvenile literature. | Internet
    industry--United States--Juvenile literature. | Online social networks--Juvenile
    literature. | Internet security measures--Juvenile literature.
 Classification: DDC 658.872--dc23
LC record available at /http://lccn.loc.gov/2016936498

Contents

What Is Pinterest? 4

Pinterest Site Bytes 6

Supplies 8

Staying Safe. 9

Giant Pin. 10

Pin Cookbook. 12

Mini Pinboard 14

Pin Lab .17

Project Pin Calendar 20

Content Creator 24

Portrait Board. 28

Glossary 31

Websites 31

Index 32

What Is **Pinterest?**

It's a summer afternoon and you're hanging out with friends. One gets the idea for a project. She wants to tie-dye some T-shirts! None of you are sure what supplies to get or what steps to take. You find an adult to help you search on Pinterest. The adult logs in to the site and types "tie-dye shirts" in the search bar. A list of ideas and projects appears. You and your friends choose the project with the brightest colors. Then you follow the directions and start making your supercool new shirts! This is the spirit of Pinterest.

Pinterest is an idea-sharing website and app. Users find articles, images, recipes, crafts, and more on the Internet. They post this content to their Pinterest profiles, where each item becomes a pin. Users can connect with each other to see one another's pins. Then, they can repin other users' content to their own Pinterest profiles.

Pinterest users create different boards for their pins. Pinners organize and name their boards by topic, event, color, and more. Pinterest's mission is to inspire people to find and share things that interest them. The site connects creators, thinkers, and doers across the globe!

Pinterest
Site Bytes

Purpose: sharing ideas

Type of Service: website and app
URL: www.pinterest.com
App name: Pinterest

Date of Founding: March 2010

Founders: Ben Silbermann, Paul Sciarra, and Evan Sharp

Compatible Devices:

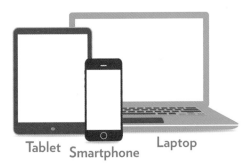

Tablet Smartphone Laptop

Tech Terms:

Pin
Pins are the images that make up Pinterest. When users find content they want to post, they turn it into pins. This is called pinning. A pin includes an image on the user's board and a link to the website where the original content is located.

Repin
If a user visits another user's Pinterest profile, he or she can repost that user's pins to his or her own Pinterest profile. This is called repinning.

Board
Boards are how Pinners organize pins. Users can name and organize their boards as they like. The group of boards a user creates makes up his or her Pinterest profile.

Founding **Pinterest**

Pinterest was created by Ben Silbermann, Paul Sciarra, and Evan Sharp. Silbermann had the original idea for the site. As a child, Silbermann loved collecting and displaying objects. In 2009, he got the idea to create a way to do this **online**. He asked Sciarra to help.
Around this time, Silbermann and Sciarra met Evan Sharp, a website designer. They asked Sharp to help work on Pinterest. Sharp put together 50 different designs before the three men settled on a final **version**. The trio's hard work paid off. Pinterest was officially launched in March 2010. By July 2013, Pinterest had 70 million users. Today, it has more than 100 million.

Paul Sciarra

Ben Silbermann

Evan Sharp

Account Info:

- Users must be at least 13 to create an account.

- Once a user creates an account, he or she chooses a username and **uploads** a profile photo.

- Only users logged in to their accounts can view, like, repin, or comment on Pinterest content.

- Users find other Pinners to follow, searching for them by name, username, or topic.

- Users can create secret boards. Users can invite specific people to view a secret board. Otherwise, only the user can see his or her secret boards.

- If a user pins something to a nonsecret board, anyone logged in to Pinterest can view it.

7

Supplies

Here are some of the materials, tools, and devices you'll need to do the projects in this book.

cardboard

corkboard

index cards

hole punch

notebook

string

printer (loaded with paper and ink)

scissors

round magnets

craft glue

pushpins

tablet

smartphone

Staying Safe

The Internet is a great resource for information. And using it can be a lot of fun! But staying safe **online** is most important. Follow these tips to use social media safely.

* Never try to sign up for a social media account if you are underage. Pinterest users must be at least 13 years old.

* Don't share personal information online, especially information people can use to find you in real life. This includes your telephone number and home address.

* Be kind online! Remember that real people post content on the Internet. Do not post rude, hurtful, or mean comments. Report any instances of **cyberbullying** you see to a trusted adult.

* In addition to cyberbullying, report any **inappropriate** content to a trusted adult.

Safety Symbols

Some projects in this book require searching on the Internet. Others require the use of hot tools. That means these projects need some adult help. Determine if you'll need help on a project by looking for these safety symbols.

 Hot!
This project requires use of a hot tool.

 Internet Use
This project requires searching on the Internet.

9

Giant Pin

Turn your refrigerator into a Pinterest board!

What you need

» round glass that is wider at the top than the bottom
» cardboard
» pencil
» scissors
» toilet paper tube
» newspaper
» acrylic paint
» foam brush
» hot glue gun & glue sticks
» 4 to 6 round magnets
» aluminum foil

1. Trace the top and bottom of the glass onto the cardboard. Cut out the two circles. Cut the toilet paper tube in half.

2. Cover your work surface with newspaper. Paint one half of the tube and both circles. Let the paint dry.

3. Hot glue a circle to each end of the tube.

4. **Stack** the magnets. Wrap aluminum foil around the magnets.

5. Glue the stack to the larger circle. Let the glue dry.

6. Make more giant pins. Use them to pin photos, recipes, and more to your refrigerator or locker.

11

Pin Cookbook

Create a cookbook for collections
of cool recipes!

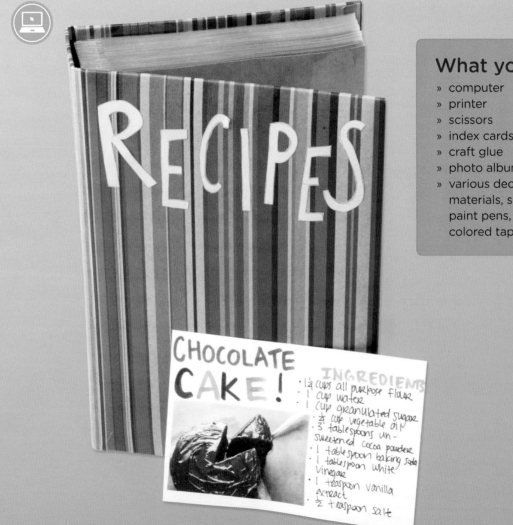

What you need

» computer
» printer
» scissors
» index cards
» craft glue
» photo album
» various decorating
  materials, such as markers,
  paint pens, stickers, ribbon &
  colored tape

Recipes and meal planning are popular Pinterest board topics. Construct a real-life collection of Internet recipes inspired by Pinterest boards!

1. Have an adult help you search **online** for recipes. Choose three recipes each for breakfast, lunch, dinner, and **dessert**.

2. Print out the recipes. Cut out the text and glue the recipes to index cards. One recipe may require several index cards. Glue a photo of the finished dish to an index card. Add the list of ingredients next to it.

3. Create index-card title pages to divide your cookbook into sections. Use "Breakfasts," "Lunches," "Dinners," and "Desserts." Or, come up with your own section names!

4. Decorate the index cards and the photo album. Think of a title for your cookbook. Write it on the cover and **spine**.

5. Put the recipes in the album. Add more recipes as you find new ones you want to try. Have fun cooking your Pinterest-inspired recipes!

Mini Pinboard

Arrange collections of photos, projects, and plans on mini pinboards!

What you need

» photos
» old magazines
» computer
» printer
» ribbon
» scissors
» small corkboard
» pushpins
» various decorating materials, such as string, buttons, dried leaves or flowers, key chains, stickers & colored paper

Pinterest boards help users plan and organize ideas. Create physical **versions** of these boards to hang in your room or in your locker. They will inspire you to dream up new ideas, make plans, or just collect your favorite things!

1. Choose a theme for your board. This could be a favorite event, sport, hobby, or animal.

2. Collect photos, **memorabilia**, and other items related to your theme. These could include personal photos or images cut from old magazines.

3. Ask an adult to help you find images or quotes **online**. Print out ones you want to include on your board.

4. Cut pieces of ribbon as long as the sides of the corkboard. Pin them to the board to form a decorative border.

(continued on the next page)

5

6

5. Pin the photos next. Try making separate sections for different aspects of the theme. For example, the theme might be birthday parties. One section could be about parties you've attended. Another section could be about parties you've hosted. A third section could feature ideas for future parties.

6. Decorate your board. Add ribbons, balloons, stickers, and more. Choose materials related to your theme.

7. Hang up your board where you will see it often.

8. Keep adding new images, activities, or inspiration to your board. Create more boards as you dream up new ideas!

#funfact
In 2015, 88 percent of Pinterest users purchased a product they had pinned.

Pin Lab

Design a perfect pin out of your favorite project!

What you need

- » computer
- » printer
- » scissors
- » poster board
- » craft glue
- » markers
- » ruler
- » pushpins
- » corkboard that is larger than the poster board
- » sticky note

Many companies and celebrities have Pinterest profiles. They want to expose their products or work to Pinterest users who are consumers and fans. These Pinners want their pins to be viewed and repinned as much as possible. Try creating a pin poster that will attract attention. Let viewers use pushpins to like and repin it.

1. Have an adult help you search **online** for a fun activity, craft, or experiment to use for your pin.

2. Print a picture to represent your project. Choose an image that is exciting or might create a lot of attention. You could also draw a picture to use.

3. Cut out the picture. Glue it to the top half of the poster board.

4. Create a title for your pin. Think of one that will draw the most interest. Write the title below the picture.

5. Under the title, write a **caption** that **describes** your pin. Think of words that might make the project or activity sound fun or interesting. The caption should be just one or two sentences.

6. Use a ruler to draw two large boxes beneath the **caption**. Label one box "Repin" and the other "Like."

7. Use pushpins to hang your pin on the corkboard.

8. Write "Voting Pins" on a sticky note. Put the note under the poster. Stick 10 to 20 pushpins into the note.

9. Have friends and family members view your pin and vote on whether they like it or want to repin it. How successful was your pin?

#funfact
There are more than 1 billion Pinterest boards. They have more than 50 billion pins.

6

8

Project Pin Calendar

Craft a calendar that will motivate you to try new activities all year long!

What you need

- » 14 sheets of card stock
- » hole punch
- » string
- » scissors
- » pencil
- » ruler
- » markers
- » computer
- » printer
- » photos
- » glue stick
- » hot glue gun & glue sticks
- » various decorating materials, such as ribbon, stickers, foam letters, feathers & more

Pinners often use Pinterest to gather ideas for activities, experiments, crafts, or projects they want to try. Find 12 activities or projects you want to try. Turn them into a calendar, with one item featured each month. Follow your calendar to complete one new craft or activity every month of the year!

1. Punch three holes along one long edge of a sheet of card stock. Use this sheet as a **template** to punch holes in the other sheets of card stock.

2. Cut three short pieces of string. **Stack** the sheets of card stock so the holes line up. Tie a string through each hole. Tie them loosely, so the pages can turn.

3. Lay the calendar down with the strings at the top. Open the first page.

4. Write the month at the top of the bottom page. Then use a ruler and pencil to draw a **grid**. Make it five rows tall and seven rows wide. Write the days of the week above the seven rows.

5. Find a calendar for reference. Copy the days of the month into your grid.

(continued on the next page)

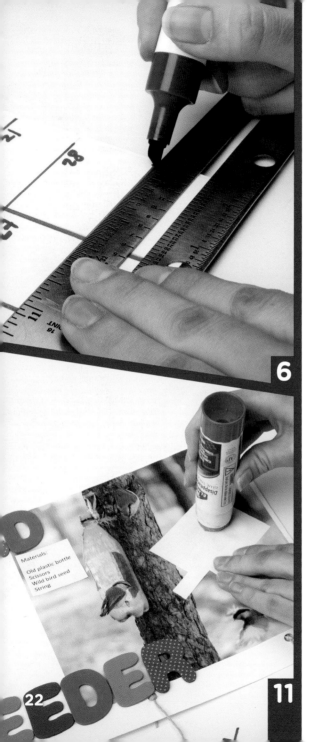

6. Trace over the pencil with a marker.

7. Turn to the next page. Repeat steps 4 through 6 for the next month. Continue repeating these steps to create a page for each month of the year.

8. Select 12 recipes, projects, crafts, or experiments you would love to try. Ask an adult to help you search **online**. Or look for ideas in magazines and books or on television. And try asking friends and family members for ideas.

9. Gather or create images for each of your choices. These could be images you find online with adult help. Or cut pictures out of old magazines. You could also draw pictures or take your own photos.

10. Print out or write down the instructions for each of your projects or activities.

11. Arrange the photos and instructions for each month's project on the page above its **grid**. Glue them in place.

12. Decorate your calendar. Add drawings, stickers, and other items that relate to each month's project. Be creative!

13. Mark special days on the calendar. This could include holidays, birthdays, vacations, and more.

14. On each page, punch a hole in the center of the edge across from the binding. Make sure the holes line up. Use these holes to hang up your calendar.

15. Have fun trying new things throughout the year!

#funfact
Pinterest is the third-most popular social networking site, after Twitter and Facebook.

Content Creator

Dream up a project and make it into a pin. See if your friends and family members can complete your project!

1. Gather peanut butter, jelly, bread, a knife, and a cup.

2. Spread peanut butter on one piece of bread.

...her piece of ...of the jelly.

3. Spread jelly on top of the peanut butter.

...p lip into ...ich. Hold 30 seconds.

Tear off crust. Remove cup. Enjoy your Pocket PBJ!

What you need

- » notebook
- » pencil
- » camera, tablet, or smartphone
- » computer
- » word-processing program
- » printer
- » scissors
- » index cards
- » clear tape
- » markers

Pinners often share ideas and projects from other Pinners or websites. But many post original ideas they've thought up! How do these Pinners communicate their ideas? What words and photos make their projects easy to complete? Become a content creator and find out!

1. Think of a simple recipe, project, or activity that you want to teach others. This could be how to create a puzzle, how to tie a **scarf**, or how to make a sandwich.

2. Think about how you would explain the project. Write the instructions in a notebook. Divide the instructions into steps. Write down a photo idea for each step.

3. Create the step photos. Do the project yourself. Take a picture of each step as you do it. The photo should show clearly how to do the step.

4. Transfer the photos to a computer. Drag the images onto a word-processing page. Use the program's editing tools to make each photo small enough to fit on an index card. Print the photos. Cut them out.

(continued on the next page)

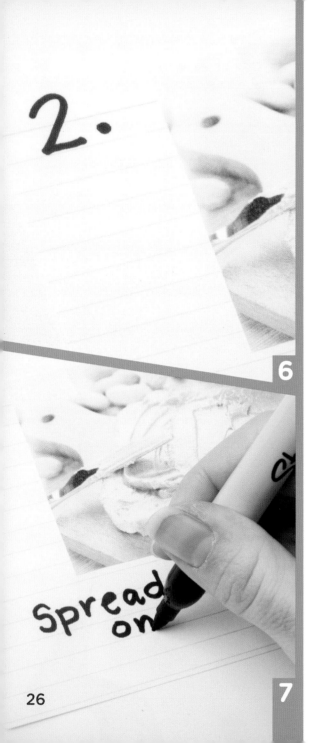

6

7

5. Tape each step photo to an index card.

6. Write the step number next to each photo.

7. Write each step's instructions under its photo.

8. Arrange the cards in order vertically. Tape the bottom edge of the first card to the top edge of the second. Leave a small space between the cards. Continue until all the cards are taped together.

9. Turn the cards over. Tape the edges together along the back sides.

10. Fold the cards back and forth into a **stack**. The back of the step 1 card should be on top. Choose a title for the project. Write it on the back of the step 1 card.

11. Give your pin to a friend or family member. Watch as he or she follows your instructions. Did your pin successfully explain the project?

9

10

27

#funfact
In 2015, the US cities where Pinterest was used most were:
- New York, New York
- Atlanta, Georgia
- Los Angeles, California
- Seattle, Washington
- San Francisco, California

Portrait Board

Pin everything about you in one place!

JORDAN

my cool dogs →

skateboarding ←

Places I want to see ↓

Best Recipes →

What you need

- » poster board
- » markers
- » photos & drawings
- » computer
- » printer
- » scissors
- » craft glue
- » colored paper

When a user posts something on Pinterest, he or she chooses a board to pin it to. Eventually, the user's profile contains a series of pinboards that represent the user's interests. Construct a poster-board Pinterest profile that contains all the things that represent you best!

1. Write your name across the top of the poster board.

2. Search for pictures of places you have been or activities you have done. If you look **online**, have an adult help you. Find drawings you have created, or take photos of collections you keep. Find or draw images of whatever makes you *you*!

3. Print any photos you took or found online. Cut out the photos.

4. Organize the images you collected into **categories**. These could be favorite things, pets, friends, and more. Each category will be a board on your profile. For each category, choose one larger image and three to four smaller images.

(continued on the next page)

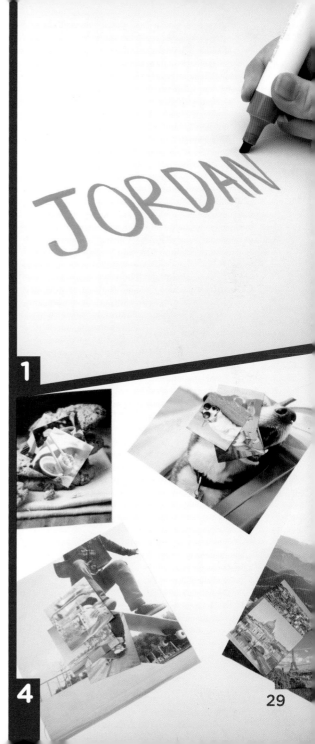

5. Arrange the photos on the poster board. Put each group in a different area. Leave some space to add more pictures later.

6. Glue the photos to the poster board.

7. Create titles for the boards on your profile. Cut strips of paper and glue one next to each board. Write the titles on the paper strips. They could be "Places I Want to See," "My Cool Dogs," or whatever matches your boards. Be creative!

8. Hang your Pinterest profile in your room. Add new pins whenever you like!

#funfact
In 2015, 58 percent of pins were pinned on a tablet, 30 percent were on a smartphone, and 12 percent were on a computer.

Glossary

caption – a written explanation of an image, such as a photo.

category – a group of things that have something in common.

cyberbully – to tease, hurt, or threaten someone online.

describe – to tell about something with words or pictures.

dessert – a sweet food, such as fruit, ice cream, or a pastry, served after a meal.

grid – a pattern with rows of squares, such as a checkerboard.

inappropriate – not suitable, fitting, or proper.

memorabilia – objects that are collected because they are related to a particular event, organization, or person.

online – connected to the Internet.

scarf – a long piece of cloth worn around the neck for decoration or to keep warm.

spine – the part of a book cover where the pages are attached.

stack – 1. to put things on top of each other. 2. a pile of things placed one on top of the other.

template – a shape or pattern used to make the same shape or pattern on something else.

upload – to transfer data from a computer to a larger network.

version – a different form or type of an original.

Websites

To learn more about Cool Social Media, visit **booklinks.abdopublishing.com**. These links are routinely monitored and updated to provide the most current information available.

Index

A

adult help, 4, 9, 13, 15, 18, 21, 22, 29

C

calendar, project for, 20, 21, 22, 23
captions, 18, 19
categories, 30
cookbook, project for, 12, 13

G

giant pin, project for, 10, 11

I

Internet
    safety, 9
    searching, 13, 18, 22, 29

M

mini pinboard, project for, 14, 15, 16

P

pinboard, project for, 14, 15, 16
Pinterest
    content, 4, 6, 7, 9, 24, 25
    history, 6, 7
    liking, 7, 18, 19
    profiles, 4, 6, 7, 18

pocket pin, project for, 24, 25, 26, 27
portrait, project for, 28, 29, 30
poster, project for, 17, 18, 19
profile, project for, 28, 29, 30

R

repinning, 4, 6, 7, 18, 19

S

safety, 9
Sciarra, Paul, 6, 7
Sharp, Evan, 6, 7
Silbermann, Ben, 6, 7
supplies, 8

W

word processing, 24, 25